Spectrum Fairies

Diana Atehortua

Fulton Books, Inc.
Meadville, PA

Published by Fulton Books 2021

ISBN 978-1-63710-454-5 (paperback)
ISBN 978-1-63710-455-2 (digital)

Printed in the United States of America

This Book Belongs To:

_____

I dedicate this book to my Humming Bird. You are my inspiration and motivation… Cassandra, I love you, and I thank you for choosing me to be your mom… Te amo!

Mom

There once lived, some very special fairies.

They lived in an enchanted forest.

These special fairies were different.

That is...what made them unique.

These wonderful fairies are
on the autism spectrum.

There was a red fairy who
liked to fly up and down and all
around like a ballerina dancer.

The blue fairy always put his favorite stones in a row like an army before the battle.

The yellow fairy never said a word...but spoke with her eyes and her heart.

The green fairy liked to talk and always repeated everything she said...over and over again.

The purple fairy just ate nuts...
That is all she liked to eat.

The other fairies in the forest
couldn't understand why they
were so different from them.

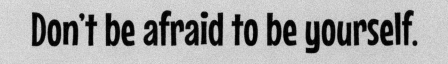

Don't be afraid to be yourself.

Do you want to be my friend?
Come play with me.

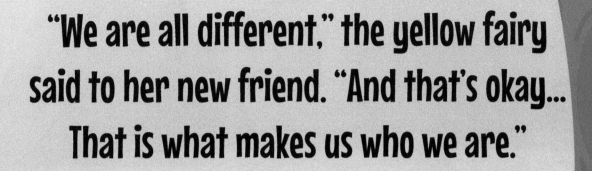

"We are all different," the yellow fairy said to her new friend. "And that's okay... That is what makes us who we are."

The other fairies are confused and
scared to be your friend... But now
I see that they are wrong.

You are the coolest fairy I ever met. It is like you said, "It's okay to be different... That is what makes us all special..."

What adventure should we go on?
Let's play the dragon game.

Okay! I am so glad we became friends.

About the Author

Diana Atehortua is an ABA therapist and the proud mother of a beautiful, smart, funny, and phenomenal daughter who is on the autism spectrum. She inspired her to become a therapist and write this book. She is her hero!

CPSIA information can be obtained
at www.ICGtesting.com
Printed in the USA
BVHW021637130721
611840BV00020B/1002

9 781637 104545